ADVENTURE
AND FAITH

RISKTAKERS

ADVENTURE

AND FAITH

LINDA
FINLAYSON

CF4·K

10 9 8 7 6 5 4 3 2 1
© Copyright 2009 Linda Finlayson
Christian Focus Publications
ISBN: 978-1-84550-491-5

Published by Christian Focus Publications,
Geanies House, Fearn, Tain, Ross-shire,
IV20 1TW, Scotland, U.K.
www.christianfocus.com
email:info@christianfocus.com

Cover design by Daniel van Straaten
Cover illustration by Neil Reed

Character and chapter illustrations by Neil Reed
Maps by Fred Apps
Printed and bound in Denmark
by Norhaven A/S

Scripture quotations are from The Holy Bible, English Standard
Version, copyright © 2001 by Crossway Bibles, a division of Good
News Publishers. Used by permission. All rights reserved.

For
George Ginther,
my Father

CONTENTS

LET'S GET STARTED

Have you ever looked at a collage? A collage is a large picture made up of a group of smaller pictures pasted around each other. When you stand back from it, you can see the pattern. It could be pictures of animals, people or buildings all joined together. But when you get closer to the collage, you can see the actual pieces that were used to make those bigger pictures. There are lots of different colours and shapes all pasted together. Without those smaller pieces, the collage would have no pattern at all.

History is a bit like that. When we look back at all the people that lived before us and the things that happened, we can see the pattern of how our country came to be. And then when we look closely at the actual people's stories who lived back then, we can see all the pieces that came together to make the big pattern. And so it is with the history of God's kingdom here on earth.

All through the Bible we read about people who either chose to follow God or reject him. We read about the wonderful ways God rescued and helped his people and the great blessings they enjoyed. And that has continued right up until today.

In these next chapters you will read about men who loved God and wanted to serve him even when it became difficult or dangerous. Each of these people lived at a different time in history and in different countries. They spoke different languages and dressed in different clothing. But they all had one thing in common. They loved God above all else. They asked God to give them courage and he did.

So come on an adventure. Read about men who faced a death sentence, travelled in a dangerous wilderness, freed slaves, smuggled Bibles past armed guards, built a city in enemy territory and faced a murderous mob all to serve God.

MARTIN LUTHER

Martin Luther lived from 1483-1546 in the country we now call Germany. When Martin was a young man he made a promise to God to become a monk if God would protect him through an especially dangerous storm. When Martin survived the storm he became a monk, but he wasn't happy. He tried very hard to serve God by obeying all the rules of the monastery, but he could find no peace in his heart. While he was there he began to study the

Bible and the writings of early Christian leaders. He became a priest and a professor, but none of this made him happy until he realised that none of his hard work would save his soul. Only by trusting in Jesus to forgive his sins did Martin find peace. With joy Martin began to teach his students and congregation about how they could be saved by faith in God and not through works. As Martin studied the scriptures more and more, he began to realise that the church leaders were teaching wrong doctrine to the people. So he began to write books challenging the church leaders and that got him into a lot of trouble.

ON TRIAL

1521

The court clerk shouted 'Silence!' as more and more people crowded noisily into the audience room of the bishop's palace. He stood with his arms folded across his black tunic and cloak, sternly waiting to be obeyed.

Martin Luther stood in front of the clerk, dressed in his monk's habit, his hands folded quietly in opposite sleeves. His head was bowed, showing his cleanly shaven tonsure. Behind Martin the important officials and landowners of the city of Worms ceased their restless chattering and turned their attention to the court that the clerk was calling to order.

When the room quieted Martin looked up at the judges arrayed before him. Emperor Charles V, a thin young man of only twenty-one, sat on a golden throne under a canopy of red velvet. On either side of the Emperor sat the Electors of Germany, the rulers of each of the German states. All were dressed in regal robes, some staring at him with unfriendly faces.

But Luther looked to the Elector of Saxony, known as Frederick the Wise, a beefy man with a thick curly gray beard and kind eyes. He was one of Martin's supporters in this room full of men who wished to condemn him to death.

Martin swallowed hard, trying to swallow away the fear that was eating away inside of him.

A man dressed in red robes rose from his seat to one side of the Emperor and the Electors. Acting as the Emperor's spokesperson, he pointed at the wooden table before Martin, full of books and pamphlets and said, 'Are these your writings?'

Martin looked down at the piles of books and then up again at his accuser. 'They are,' he replied as steadily as he could manage.

'Do you renounce all that you have written in these books?' the prosecutor demanded ferociously.

Martin stared at him, his heart pounding, sweat beginning to pour down the back of his neck. The room had gone completely silent as they awaited his reply. Martin remained silent too. He thought about all that had led up to this moment.

He had become a monk to honour a promise he had made to God as a young man. And he had studied to become a lecturer at the university in Wittenberg with the encouragement of the Elector of Saxony.

As he had studied the Scriptures he had come to realize that salvation comes only through faith in God, not through trying to be and do good. He had begun to teach what he found in the Bible. Slowly he had come to realize that the Pope had taught the church errors that needed to be corrected, and so he began to write books and pamphlets to let people know the truth.

Not surprisingly, the Pope and many who served in the church were not happy. And neither were those like the princes or the emperor who agreed with the Pope in order to keep peace in their lands. Only the Elector of Saxony had had the courage to offer Martin protection and encouragement; until now, when it had all been taken out of his hands by Martin himself.

A month ago Martin had received a letter summoning him to the city of Worms, where the church and state leaders were meeting to discuss government matters. Full of confidence, he had agreed to come, certain he could speak out strongly for the truths of God. The journey to Worms had been heartening. All along the way, people had turned out to wave and shout their support as his wooden cart travelled through their towns and cities. But now that he stood in the very presence of the Emperor and great leaders of Germany, Martin felt his courage desert him, leaving him shaking and afraid to speak.

'Do you renounce these writings?' the prosecutor demanded again.

Martin swallowed and spoke. 'May I have time to pray and consider my answer?' he asked.

His accuser snorted his disgust, but looked to the emperor for an answer. Emperor Charles hesitated for a moment and then nodded. 'He may have until tomorrow afternoon when we will all meet here again.'

Martin bowed his head to keep everyone from seeing the tears of relief that had formed in his eyes. He allowed the soldiers, who stepped forward at the emperor's signal, to lead him away quietly to the house up the street where he was lodging.

Martin spent an agonizing night in prayer and pacing. He knew if he said no to the emperor he would be condemned to death. But if he said yes, then he would be denying God and condemning his soul. Martin knew what he had to do, but he also knew he needed courage from God to do it. All night long Martin prayed that God would take away the terrible fear that was eating away at his insides and give him peace. And as the sun rose the next morning, God answered his prayer. The terrible fear began to melt away and in its place God gave him the quiet certainty that He was with Martin and would keep him in perfect peace.

Once more the soldiers marched Martin down the street to the Bishop's palace and once more Luther stood before the church and his royal accusers. Even more people had squeezed into the audience room, causing the temperature to rise and Martin to begin sweating. But God's peace remained in his heart, so that when the prosecutor demanded once more that Martin renounce his writings, Martin was ready to answer.

'My writings fall into three categories,' he began, ignoring the angry look on the emperor's face. 'There are books here that teach theology and doctrine that even the Pope has approved. So I do not renounce those because we all agree they teach the truth. But I have also written books against the Pope's wrong teachings. I cannot renounce these because I believe them to be true. And finally I have written some pamphlets against certain individuals, leaders who I believe are deliberately leading God's people astray. I admit some of those writings have been unkind and were written in anger. I regret that I used such tones. However, I do not regret that I spoke out against their errors.'

Emperor Charles waved his hand impatiently. 'I don't want to hear long speeches. Answer the charges. Do you recant your writings?'

Martin stood up to his full height and answered with confidence. 'Since your Imperial Majesty requests a simple, plain answer here it is. Unless you can prove to me through God's Word that I'm wrong, then I cannot and will not renounce what I have written. May God help me.'

The crowds of people began to buzz, some angry, some cheering softly. The Emperor rose angrily from his throne and ordered Martin to be taken from the room. He dismissed the court and swept out of the audience room with his courtiers rushing after him.

As Martin was led through the streets, word of what had happened spread through the town. People poured into the streets cheering Martin as he passed but kept well back from the guards. Martin waved and called out to some. He felt relieved that the trial was finished; thrilled that God had given him the courage to speak out so clearly. But he also knew it was not over. The Emperor had yet to pronounce judgment on him and there was only one judgment for anyone who defied the Pope...death.

But it didn't happen right away. Instead Martin remained imprisoned in the house for a week wondering what would happen next. And he was allowed visitors. Among those who came to either congratulate him on his courage or try to persuade him to change his mind, was Elector Philip of Hesse.

Martin stood up and bowed respectfully when Elector Philip entered dressed in a tunic of rich red brocade and a fur-trimmed cloak.

'Sit, sit,' Philip said after seating himself by the fireplace. 'I had to come and see the man who had the courage to say no to the Pope. Tell me, are you sorry you have made your stand for God's truth?'

Martin shook his head. 'I couldn't deny God. Although now I can't help worrying about what will happen next. Why has the Emperor not called me back to pronounce judgment?'

Philip smiled. 'An excellent question. First I believe he was hoping if given time you would change your mind. Now, however, I have heard he is bargaining with the Pope over some land he wants the Pope to give him. Only after the Emperor gets what he wants will he then pronounce the sentence against you.'

Martin shook his head. 'So these decisions have more to do with politics than God's truth? The church and the Emperor are more corrupt than I thought.'

'Do not fear,' Philip assured him. 'I have secured safe passage for you for the next twenty days to visit your family and friends while the great men argue with each other. And the Elector of Saxony has provided you with money for your travels. You may leave tomorrow with my herald who will declare that anyone who harms you will have to answer to me. My twenty horsemen should also help.' He leaned back in his chair with a satisfied smile.

Martin was overwhelmed with the offer and thanked the Elector. Philip waved aside Martin's words. 'I find you an interesting man and I plan to read some of your books. Now you should plan to be gone at first light. No point calling too much attention to your leaving.'

Over the next few days Martin and a few of his friends travelled to various cities in Germany, giving Martin an opportunity to preach and teach as well as say farewell to his many supporters. Each day Martin expected to hear that the emperor had pronounced him excommunicated from the church and the rest of society. Once that happened Martin would become an outlaw. Anyone who helped Martin in any way, either feeding him or giving him a place to live, would be killed. And anyone was free to kill Martin without any fear that they would go to prison or be executed.

Slowly the group of friends dropped off, leaving Martin with only two friends who accompanied him to the town of Mohra to visit Martin's Uncle Heinz.

Even the herald and the horsemen given to Martin by the Elector of Hesse returned home. So when the three men left the town in their cart, they were unprotected and unprepared for the attack.

As they entered a wooded area near the ruins of a chapel, suddenly a small band of armed horsemen charged at them. Martin and his friends had no weapons to defend themselves. All Martin could think to do was reach for his knapsack that contained his New Testament and his Hebrew Bible before he was grabbed by one of the horsemen and thrown across the horse's neck in front of the rider. Out of the corner of his eye he saw one of his friends leap into the bushes away from a raised sword. He couldn't see the other one, but he could hear him shouting at the attackers. Martin was relieved to know his friends were alive as the group rode off with him bouncing on the horse in a most undignified position.

At first Martin was unsure if he was with friends or foes. His captors didn't talk to him, but did allow him to sit upright on an extra horse they had with them. He was hemmed in on all sides as they travelled across the wooded countryside. They stayed away from the well travelled road and took cover whenever people came into view. But they were not unkind to Martin. They gave him food and water and stopped to rest occasionally. Martin worried that the Emperor had already pronounced judgment on him and these men

were planning to kill him. But why had they not done so right away? Why this long journey on horseback?

As the sun began to set, the group came to a small cottage where they stopped and Martin was ordered to go inside. Uneasy, but not wanting to anger his captors, he did as he was told. The leader of the group followed Martin in and closed the door.

'We are from Elector Frederick,' he said quickly. 'We are to take you to the Wartburg castle tonight, but you must go in disguise. Everyone knows what Dr. Martin Luther looks like, so you must change into the clothing on the table. Hurry! We still have a long way to go.'

Too surprised for words, Martin looked at the pile of clothing. Shaking them out he realized he would be trading his monk's clothing for a knight's. But not a very important knight. The doublet, hose and cloak were worn and patched. All the better not to call attention to himself. It took a few minutes more than the leader wanted for Martin to change. This type of clothing was unfamiliar to him since he had worn a monk's simple long tunic and cloak most of his adult life. Finally Martin buckled his belt across his brown tunic and threw the dark green cloak about his shoulders.

'Put on the hat,' the leader ordered. 'Otherwise people will see your tonsure and know you are not a poor knight. You would be wise to grow your hair and beard to further your disguise.'

'But how long will I have to remain hidden at Wartburg?' Martin asked, thinking how long it would take to grow his beard.

The leader shrugged. 'A good long time, I should think. The Pope and the Emperor aren't going to give up hunting you any time soon. Come, we must leave now.'

They rode on for the rest of the evening through more woods and finally arrived at the grey stone castle. Inside the strong walls, Martin dismounted from his horse finally feeling safe.

'Knight George,' the castellan called out as he walked across the courtyard to Martin. 'Welcome. Your rooms are ready, if you will come this way,' he said with a smile.

Knight George. So this was to be his new name for a while. Martin returned the smile but said nothing. No one here must know who he really was for his and their safety. The Elector Fredrick the Wise had been very wise indeed with his secret arrangements. Perhaps here, in peace and safely, Martin could spend some time translating the Bible into the German language. He wanted everyone in his country to be able to read God's word in their own language.

Devotional Thought:

*He rescued me from my strong enemy and from those
who hated me, for they were too mighty for me...but the
LORD was my support. He brought me out into a broad
place; he rescued me, because he delighted in me.*

Psalm 18:17-19

David, the Psalmist, wrote these words to praise
God for his help. God had helped him to defeat his
enemy. He did this because he was pleased with
David. How do we please God? By trusting and
obeying him.

Martin would have read these words and thought
about his enemies, the Pope and the Emperor. He
had told both those powerful men they were wrong
about God. It would have been safer to keep quiet but
Martin spoke up, knowing that God was his support.
God used Martin to bring about the reformation of
the entire church.

Martin stayed in hiding for over a year translating
the Bible into German so that his fellow Germans
could read God's Word for themselves. His writings
influenced a great many people and slowly the
Protestant church came into being. Martin was able
to return to Wittenberg where he married and started
a family. Martin took a risk for God and God gave
him courage and blessing.

GERMANY

FACT FILE

The nation of Germany is often on the news and it is certainly in your history books. But in Martin Luther's time Germany as we know it today didn't even exist. It was originally a collection of tribes which then later became a group of states ruled by princes and an Emperor. In the 1800s the German Confederation was formed - a loose league of thirty-nine sovereign states. It wasn't until 1871 that the state known as Germany was unified and the German Empire was formed. After the two world wars Germany was again split in 1945 into two nations - West and East Germany. In 1990 after mass demonstrations in the Communist East both West and East Germany were reunited to form one nation again.

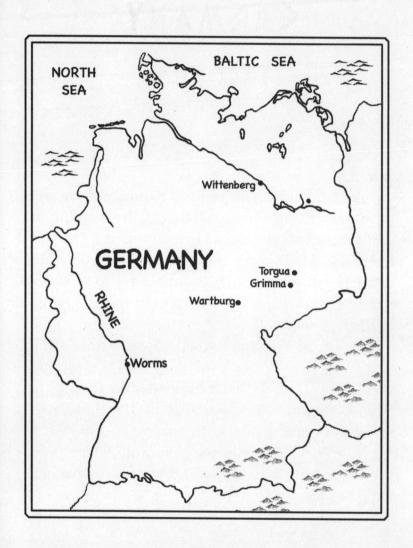

NORTH
SEA

BALTIC SEA

Wittenberg

GERMANY

RHINE

Torgua
Grimma

Wartburg

Worms

DAVID BRAINERD

David Brainerd lived from 1718–47. He was born in Haddam, Connecticut in the United States.

David's parents died when he was young and he went to live with a local pastor. When David turned twenty-one he was converted and felt a call to become a missionary. After some training at university, David was approved by the Missionary Society of Scotland to be a missionary to the North American Indians. At this time the United States was not its own country. Instead it was made up of small British colonies along the east coast of North America. European people had been settling in the land for over one hundred years now and forcing the North American Indians to move further inland. There were no roads to the Indian villages; only rivers and pathways through the dense forests and over mountains. Many people were also fearful of the Indians because some tribes had killed some of the settlers. But for the most part, the Indian tribes preferred to pursue their own way of life away from the Europeans. David became burdened for the many Indian tribes and planned a number of dangerous trips to share the gospel with them.

DANGER IN THE MOUNTAINS

OCTOBER-NOVEMBER 1744

D arkness was settling in as the small group of weary travellers reached the wayside cabin. It was more of a shack with just four log walls and a plank roof, but the men were glad of the shelter from the cold autumn air and the gathering rain clouds. David Brainerd and Eliab Byram tethered their horses to allow them to graze near the cabin while their three Delaware Indian guides gathered wood to make a small fire.

'This hasn't been so bad,' Eliab said, straightening up his long coat and loosening his neckerchief. 'A hard ride, but we must have covered twenty-five miles.'

'Tomorrow will be harder,' David warned. Then he began to cough, a deep hurting cough that made it difficult for him to breath. After a few minutes the coughing subsided and David was able to breath once more.

'Are you alright?' Eliab asked. He knew David had a weak chest and sometimes coughed up blood.

David waved aside his friend's concern. 'I'll be fine after a night's rest.' Then he patted his mare affectionately and followed Eliab to the cabin.

After a supper of hard cheese and bread with cold water from a nearby stream, they warmed themselves by the fire and then stretched out on the dirt floor to sleep, wrapped in their warm cloaks.

David and Eliab were ministers from New England, travelling through the mountains of Pennsylvania to preach the gospel, the good news about Jesus Christ, to tribes along the Susquehanna River, many miles away. Tattamy, their interpreter and his two friends were their guides through the largely unexplored mountain wilderness. They were an interesting looking group; three Delaware Indians dressed in deerskin leggings, boots and capes and shaved heads with only scalp locks hanging down their backs, and the two New Englanders dressed in shirts, wool weskits, tight-fitting trousers and long coats.

The next morning they all rose at dawn. David was stiff and cold. He wrapped his cloak tightly around himself as he headed out into the forest. It was his custom to pray in the woods because he found that the quietness of the forest kept him focused on his prayers. But he was careful not to wander too far and become lost as he walked and talked with God. He asked God for safety as they travelled over the mountains and rivers yet to come, for strength to face the rest of the difficult journey and for the right words to preach to the people when they arrived at their destination.

As David returned to the cabin where Eliab and their horses waited in the brightening day, David could see the rugged mountains spread out before them. His heart sank at their height and steepness.

'Tattamy told me to meet them at that outcropping of rocks,' Eliab pointed down the hill. 'He said if we follow this trail it will take us safely down to that valley. Are you ready? Here take this dried meat. You haven't had any breakfast.'

David took the food offered to him wrapped in a handkerchief and stuffed it in his pocket. 'I'll eat it later,' he replied, mounting his mare. 'We should get moving.'

So the two men started out, their horses working their way down the hillside. After meeting up with Tattamy and the others, they began their difficult climb up the side of the steep tree covered mountains. At one point they came to a huge valley cut through the mountain range by the Lehigh River. They climbed gingerly down into the steep gorge and forded the river. Following the river along, they found a gap in the mountain range which was a welcome relief. But the relief was short lived.

They came once more to tall mountains. But instead of thick forest to work their way through, they were now faced with rocky ground. The horses struggled to get their footing on the large rocks and David and Eliab tightened their grips as their horse stumbled and righted themselves.

'What a hideous place this is,' David complained just before his mare suddenly stumbled once more.

'Neiggghhhhhhh!' the mare cried out, this time unable to regain her footing.

David was suddenly flung out of the saddle, landing on the sharp rocks.

'Ouch! Oww!' he cried.

'Neiggghhhhh!' the mare's body fell Thud! on the rocks next to him, crying in pain.

Eliab leapt off his horse and together with Tattamy ran to help David up.

'Are you alright?' Eliab asked.

David stumbled as he tried to rise, but replied, 'Yes, only bruised.' And then they all looked to where his mare lay on the rocks, one of her back legs pinned at a painful angle between two rocks. She was whinnying with pain. David picked his way quickly over to her, examined the leg and then shook his head. The leg was badly broken. He went to her head and took it in his arms, cradling her and whispering softly. They were too far from help out in the middle of the mountainous wilderness. There was only thing to do.

David looked up at his companions with tears in his eyes. 'I can't leave her in this pain.'

Tattamy nodded and walked away to tell his Indian companions what had happened. Eliab went to his own horse and took down the rifle that was fastened to his saddlebag. He handed it to David with an understanding look and then led his own horse away from the scene.

David said goodbye to his mare who had served him so well, taking him from place to place to preach to North American Indian tribes in New York, New Jersey and Pennsylvania. He would miss her. Then quickly before he could think too much about it, he cocked the rifle and shot her. The shot was true and she died instantly, no longer in pain. With a heavy heart he removed his saddlebags and saddle and then ran his hand down her mane one last time.

Eliab took the saddle and bags and loaded them on his own horse in silence. Sometimes it was best to be quiet when someone was grieving. Then together the two men started out on foot, Eliab leading his horse, following their guides to the next mountain. After a time, David spoke.

'I asked God for safety and protection this morning and he answered that prayer.'

'He did. You could have been killed back there,' Eliab agreed. 'But I'm still sorry about your horse.'

That night it turned very cold, the frost heavy on the ground. Tattamy and his companions gathered wood together to make a large fire and they huddled around it wrapped in their blankets. Before lying down on the ground to sleep, David led the small group in prayer, thanking God for safety thus far and asking for his continued protection through the night.

They travelled through the mountains and valleys for another day and a half until they finally came to the Susquehanna River. Here Tattamy led them along the wide, fast flowing river until they reached an Indian settlement. Twelve homes made of animal hides and supported on long poles stood in the clearing. Almost seventy people lived in the village. Tattamy led them to the chief, who sat outside his home with some of his advisors. Everyone else suddenly seemed to have something to do close to the council and they lingered to see these two white men in funny clothes.

David smiled at the chief and bowed his head respectfully. Through Tattamy's interpretation David introduced himself and Eliab and said they had travelled a long way to bring them good news. Interested, the chief asked them to continue.

David said he wanted to tell them about God, the creator of the world and his plan to bring salvation to mankind. The chief considered that news and after speaking with his councillors agreed that they should like to hear more of the God David worshipped. So after offering David and Eliab food and drink, the chief commanded all his people to gather by the large fire pit and hear what David had to say.

The people sat in groups. The men dressed in deerskin pants and moccasins sat in front, with young boys dressed only in deerskin loin clothes trying to sit like their fathers. Behind them sat or stood the women dressed in deerskin tunics with their dark hair tied into braids.

Speaking slowly so that Tattamy had time to translate his sentences into the Seneca language, David told them about God. David knew these people worshipped many gods so he was careful to tell them that Jehovah, the God of the Bible, was the only true and living God. The people listened politely, but when the sermon was finished they all rose and went back to their work without comment. David and Eliab felt discouraged.

'Will you and your people hear me speak to you again?' David asked the chief.

'Oh yes,' the chief responded through Tattamy's translation. 'We would like to hear more of this God of yours, but right now we must prepare for our hunt. We must make enough arrows and frames to carry our catches. We leave in two days' time. Tomorrow morning you may speak again.'

David and Eliab tried to see the good part of that speech: the chief was open to hearing the gospel. But had they travelled such a long way to have only three days to preach? It didn't seem long enough.

Over the next two days David spoke of how sin entered the world and changed God's beautiful creation. He described how God sent his son Jesus to take their punishment for their sin because he loved them. Each time the people listened quietly, but none wanted to know more or could see that the good news of the gospel could change their lives.

David also took time to visit with each family while they prepared for their hunt. The Susquehanna people were polite but not one was converted.

Discouraged, the men loaded up Eliab's horse with

their belongings and said goodbye to the Susquehanna village. Tattamy went with them acting as their guide to take them back the way they had come.

The return trip through the Pennsylvania Mountains was no easier. In fact it took longer with all of them on foot. And the weather had turned colder. As they huddled around the fire at night they could hear the wolves howling not far from where they sat. It sent a shiver up David's spine. But the wolves never came near enough to cause them any real alarm.

Arriving back at his cottage at the Forks of Delaware, David was tired and his cough was worse. He had enough strength to visit a few of the Indian villages nearby to preach and he was warmly received. One woman was in tears when she heard how Jesus had died for her and David gently led her to the Lord. Another man troubled by his sins asked David to pray for him that he might find peace with God. But even these conversions did not stop David's feelings of failure at the Susquehanna village. He worried that they might never have another opportunity to hear more about God. So he travelled to New York on a borrowed horse to attend a presbytery meeting and report on his work.

The weather turned cold and very wet and David arrived at the meeting a sick man. But he made his report and the presbytery encouraged him to go back to the Susquehanna people when his health and the season permitted. Feeling very low, David left the meeting and rode to see his friend, Aaron Burr, in Newark, New Jersey.

'Come in, come in out of the cold and wet,' Aaron greeted his friend. David stumbled in the front door of a cosy cottage coughing and shivering. 'Dear me,' his host exclaimed. 'You are too ill my friend to be riding about in this weather. You should be in bed. Come this way. Once you are settled I will send for the doctor.'

Within a short time David found himself tucked up in bed with a warmed brick at his feet and Aaron's housekeeper bringing him some hot soup. While David balanced the bowl carefully and sipped soup from his spoon, Aaron sat by his bed telling him the news of mutual friends. David smiled at his cheerful companion. All of David's family except one brother had died and David often felt lonely. Aaron's friendship made him feel like he had another brother. He knew that any time he needed someone to encourage him, Aaron was just the person. He could be cheerful and he could be serious

'You will stay here until you are well again,' Aaron declared. 'I will see to it that you receive the best care. And I want you to leave here a happier man too. Now about your so-called failures. I know you're discouraged because not all the people who hear you preach are converted right away. But that doesn't mean you have failed. You have been faithful and now you must let the Holy Spirit convince their hearts.'

David sighed and handed the soup bowl to Aaron. 'You are right. Sometimes I just worry that there isn't enough time to tell everyone. None should perish because we haven't told them. We don't know how many tribes of people there are out in that great wilderness. I just feel I shouldn't be lying here in bed when they need to know of God's love.' Then he started to cough for a long time until he fell back against the pillows exhausted.

Aaron took David's hand firmly in his. 'Your concern for the lost does you credit David, but you can't travel anywhere when you are ill. Spend time recovering here and together we will pray for your next venture into the Pennsylvania wilderness. And then in God's time you might be able to go back.'

Devotional Thought:

*For the sake of Christ, then, I am content with
weaknesses, insults, hardships, persecutions, and
calamities. For when I am weak, then I am strong.*
2 Corinthians 12:10

The apostle Paul told the Corinthian Christians that he suffered from an illness or problem that God had refused to heal. God had told Paul that he would give him the ability to live with it. Paul didn't argue with God. Instead he accepted his weakness as a chance to bring glory to God.

David Brainerd also knew about weakness. He suffered from tuberculosis, a disease of the lungs, so that he was often ill with colds and flu. He could have chosen an easier life and become a pastor at a local church. But David listened to God's call to preach to the Seneca and Delaware Indians instead.

David's journal is full of his thoughts and concerns for the native peoples and his desire to serve God. He kept travelling for three more years until he became too ill to travel. His fiancée, Jerusha Edwards, nursed him until he died at age twenty-nine. His brother, John Brainerd, then took David's place and continued gravelling to preach to the Indian tribes.

AMERICA

FACT FILE

The nation of America is also known at the United States. With about 306 million people it is the third largest country by population. The nation was founded by thirteen colonies of Great Britain that were located along the Atlantic seaboard. On July 4, 1776 these colonies issued the Declaration of Independence which proclaimed their independence from Great Britain. In 1787 they adopted a constitution which remains to this day. During the 19th century the United States acquired land from France, Spain, the United Kingdom, Mexico and Russia and annexed Texas and Hawaii. Disputes between the Northern and Southern states resulted in the Civil War of the 1860s. As a nation its motto is 'In God We Trust'.

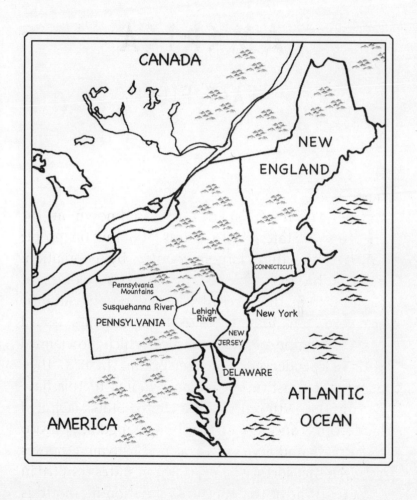

CANADA

NEW
ENGLAND

CONNECTICUT

Pennsylvania
Mountains

Susquehanna River

PENNSYLVANIA

Lehigh
River

New York

NEW
JERSEY

DELAWARE

ATLANTIC

OCEAN

AMERICA

WILLIAM KING

Willliam King lived from 1812-1895. He was born near Londonderry in Northern Ireland into a Christian home. William was the youngest of a large farming family and the one chosen to have a higher education. William was converted at sixteen and went on to university to become a teacher. When William was twenty, his entire family decided to emigrate to America and take up farming in Ohio. William went with them but then chose to travel south to Louisiana where he taught school and eventually became a headmaster. William met his wife, Mary, there and they settled down to raise a family. But God had other plans for William. He called William to be a minister. So William moved his family to Edinburgh and studied at the new Free Church College. Then he was sent as a missionary to Canada. But life didn't work out just as William had planned. God had some special work for him to do. It involved some sadness and some danger, but God was with William every step of the way.

SETTING THE SLAVES FREE
APRIL-MAY 1848

The night was hot and sticky as William stood on the wide porch of the plantation house in southern Louisiana. Noisy cicadas sang in the trees while mosquitoes buzzed about his ears. Bullfrogs joined the chorus from the pond nearby. William pushed back his dark hair and loosened the stiff collar of his white shirt. He had been away from this southern state for four years and he found the stifling heat difficult to get used to again.

Four years, he thought. How much my life has changed in that short time. Four years ago he had a wife and a son. They'd left his wife's American homeland to go to Edinburgh so William could study to become a minister. Now William had his degree and was ordained, but his wife, son and baby daughter were all dead from illness and William was alone. He had not planned to return to Louisiana after Mary died. He had been sent by the church to be a missionary in Canada, but something happened to change that.

Much to William's horror he found that he had inherited property when his wife died. Owning land in the southern United States meant owning slaves. As a minister of the gospel, William believed that he could not, should not, own other human beings. So he had come back to set matters right. If only it would be as easy as putting up a 'for sale' sign.

William sighed and straightened his collar. He had put it off long enough. Inside the beautiful colonial house sat his father-in-law's young widow and a number of plantation owners and their wives from the community. He had invited them to tell them his plans.

'Ladies and Gentlemen,' he addressed the expensively dressed group when he entered the large sitting room. The conversations slowly ceased as they turned their attention to William. William was conscious of the distressed look on Frances Emmaline's face as she stared up at him. As his father-in-law's widow and co-inheritor of the property, William had already told her his plans. She had promised to say nothing although she was very unhappy.

'I have been with you all now since last November and I have enjoyed re-acquainting myself with you all and your gracious hospitality,' he began with a smile. His neighbours nodded and returned his smile. 'And I've enjoyed being able to preach in many of the churches too. Always a great thing for a preacher to do! But I must tell you now that I will be leaving your beautiful state and the country in a few weeks.'

That caused a buzz of conversation and questions. William remained silent as they passed puzzled looks and comments between themselves. He knew what they all thought he should do. Marry Frances Emmaline, combine their two properties and run the plantation just as it had been run for years.

But William could not do that. Once, long ago, he might have. He had moved to Louisiana from Ireland to teach school. He loved the people and the slow, gracious way of life, and he had turned a blind eye to the slavery problem.

After all most of his friends were kind people and treated their slaves well, so it must be alright. But slowly William became convicted about two things: his own behaviour was not as Christ-like as it should be, and owning slaves was wrong.

He could do nothing about the second conviction at that time, but the first one was within his power to change. Both he and his wife, Mary, began to study

God's Word, desiring to have a deeper relationship with God. And it was during that time that William felt called to the ministry.

Now four years later, God had provided a way for him to deal with the slavery question. He cleared his throat and began the speech he had prepared, 'I have decided to sell my part of the property that I have inherited from my wife and her father. Frances Emmaline will keep her part. I wish to return to Canada to continue my missionary work. And,' here he offered a silent prayer for strength, 'I plan to take my slaves with me and give them their freedom.'

One of the wives dropped her wine glass and it shattered the shocked silence. Cries of 'You can't do that!' 'Are you mad?' followed as the angry plantation owners leapt to their feet.

As the noise subsided, one man's voice sounded above the rest. 'Be reasonable, William. You can't take all those darkies with you. It wouldn't be safe. Better to sell them with the land. I'll give you a thousand dollars for them!'

'You can't do this,' another man said. 'Think how this will unsettle the community, especially our slaves.'

William listened patiently but refused to change his mind. He had to do what was right. His guests left a short time later, some warning him that this matter wasn't closed.

The threat turned out to be true. William endured many visits, letters and threats from plantation owners around the parish. Many were angry because some of their slaves had already escaped to Canada and freedom even though they had been chased by slave catchers. William's action would only cause more to runaway.

William worked as quickly as he could, selling his land and farm equipment. An uncle of his wife, Dr. Phare, housed William's slaves for him keeping them safe from the threats against their lives. Then William arranged passage for himself and fourteen slaves on a steamer boat heading north up the Mississippi River.

The day before they were to leave, William gathered his slaves into a group on Dr. Phare's plantation. 'We will be leaving tomorrow on a journey that will take you to Canada and freedom,' he began. But he saw that they didn't understand what he meant. They had been slaves all their lives and now they thought William was just taking them to a new plantation to work, in a place called Canada.

'Is it far away?' Harriet, one of the slaves, asked anxiously.

'Yes, very far,' William replied. 'It will take us a week or two to get there.'

'No!' she replied and started to cry.

William was puzzled. Going to her, he put his arm around her shoulder to comfort her and asked her gently what was wrong.

'My son,' she said, still weeping. 'Solomon is only four years old and part of Mrs. Phare's property. It was alright when we lived near each other, but I can't leave him behind. Oh, Massa King, please, please, will you buy him so he can come with me?'

William's heart sank. How could he buy a slave when he was trying to set the ones he had free? But how could he ask a young mother to leave her child and never see him again? After a few minutes of thought William finally said, 'I'll see what I can do.'

Deciding that buying young Solomon was the lesser of two evils, William bought the boy for $150 and presented him to his mother the next morning.

'Thank you, Massa, thank you,' Harriet said over and over as she hugged her little boy. Solomon, glad to see his mother, endured her embraces without too much wiggling.

At the wharf, William herded his charges on the riverboat. But many people had gathered to see them go, including gun-carrying plantation owners. They said they were just there to make sure none of their slaves left with William too, but William was nervous that someone might accidentally get shot. After all it wasn't a capital crime to kill a slave. They were just

property. The owner would have to be paid for the loss, but no one considered it murder.

Fortunately no one interfered with William or his slaves and soon the riverboat was on its way up the Mississippi River. The other passengers were amazed to see such a crowd of slaves sitting and sleeping on the open foredeck of the ship. William had to listen to many people and their opinions of what he was doing. 'Don't you worry they may rise up and hurt you because you don't have a foreman with a gun travelling with you?' 'Aren't you worried they will run away when we dock to pick up more passengers?' 'It's wrong to set those people free. They need to be kept in line for their own good.' William shook his head and replied as politely as possible.

At the end of the 1500 mile journey, they had to switch to a smaller boat to take them through the canals and on to Ohio to the place that William's father and brothers farmed. So William called his slaves together by the wharf.

'Friends,' he began with a smile and held up some papers. 'I want to tell you that you are no longer my slaves. Here are the papers that tell everyone you are free men and women. You have a choice now. You may take the paper with your name on it and leave. Make a life for yourself here in this free state of Ohio. No one can enslave you here. Or you can come with me, first to my family's farm and then on to Canada where I plan to see you can buy land of your own and begin a new life there.'

The men and women looked at each other and then Stephen, their unofficial spokesperson, replied. 'Massa, we will go with you. You have kept us safe and we want to go to this place called Canada.'

'Right, then,' William replied with a wide grin. 'Let's get on board that boat and finish the journey.'

As they all climbed onto the old packet whose paint was peeling and in need of some repair, the captain stepped forward.

'How many people do you have?' he demanded.

'Fifteen plus myself,' William said.

The gruff captain pushed back his cap and said, 'Too many. I'll take the darkies but you will have to get passage elsewhere.'

Stephen turned back toward William with fear on his face. 'Massa,' he whispered. 'I don't like this. You can't leave us now.'

William hesitated. He could take the next packet boat and not be far behind, but his friends looked so frightened that he decided he should stay with them.

'Captain, I rather stay with my friends. Surely

you could find a corner for me to sleep in?' William said.

The captain stared at him. 'You'd have to bunk with the crew. Not very comfortable for a gentleman like you. I thought you would want to have a cabin to yourself.'

'Not at all,' William assured him. 'A bunk in a corner will do me fine.'

As the next leg of the journey began, William shared his story with the curious crew.

'You must be crazy or very brave,' one of them remarked. 'Few people would risk freeing their slaves these days.'

'Mind your manners,' the captain barked. 'And your language. Mr. King here's a minister.'

The crew became very respectful at once and obeyed their captain's orders to use clean language. They even attended the prayer meetings William conducted each evening after the boat docked for the night. William thanked God for the opportunity to share the gospel with these men.

When at last the tired group arrived at William's father's farm they were welcomed with joy. William knew his father and brothers were already part of the Underground Railroad, a group of people who helped runaway slaves escape from the slave catchers. So he knew he had no worries about their reaction to fifteen former slaves arriving on their doorstep.

'You have travelled a long way,' William's elderly father said. 'How pleased your mother would have been had she lived to see this. Now you must stay as long as you like and your friends too.'

'Thanks, Da,' William replied. 'I'll stay a little while, but I must return to Canada soon. I need to arrange for a place for my friends to live. If you will care for them while I'm gone, then I will return and take them home.'

And so it was agreed. William stayed a couple of weeks and preached in the churches in the area and then headed north to Canada. His friends stayed behind, housed in various homes on the King property and they attended school to learn how to read and write.

When William arrived in Toronto he was amazed at his reception. The newspapers had published several stories about William's journey with his slaves. They had called him Moses leading his people to the Promised Land. So everyone he met knew the story and when he went to the presbytery meeting he received a standing ovation. Encouraged by the enthusiastic reception, William gave a speech asking the church to help set up a community for his former slaves and others who escaped to Canada.

He outlined a plan to purchase land that they could sell to the people at cost so they could farm and support themselves. He also wanted them to help build a school and a church. After much discussion, William's plan was accepted by the presbytery and William was appointed the committee chairman.

William knew he had a lot of hard work ahead of him, but he also knew that God would give him the strength to complete it. Now, instead of being sorry that he had inherited slaves from his wife, he rejoiced that God had given him a chance to bring freedom to these people and help them build a community where they could work and serve God.

Devotional Thought:

The Spirit of the Lord GOD is upon me, because the LORD has anointed me to bring good news to the poor; he has sent me to bind up the brokenhearted, to proclaim liberty to the captives, and the opening of the prison to those who are bound; Isaiah 61:1

Isaiah wrote these words to tell the people of Israel about the coming Messiah, the One whom God would send to bring good news, heal people and give them freedom. That person was Jesus. When Jesus began his ministry on earth, he went to the synagogue one day and read out these verses to the congregation. Then he told them he was the one Isaiah had been writing about. And then Jesus did just what the prophecy had said. He told them the good news of the gospel, he healed the sick and through his death and resurrection brought freedom and peace to sinners.

William wanted to be more like Jesus. So he also preached the good news of the gospel and brought freedom to those who were slaves. With some help he was able to set up a whole town for escaped slaves with a school and a church. William lived to see the Civil War in the United States that eventually freed the slaves in that country. William continued to faithfully preach God's Word until he died.

CANADA
FACT FILE

The nation of Canada gets its name from a native Indian name Kanata meaning village or settlement. The country extends from the Atlantic Ocean in the east to the Pacific Ocean in the west and northwards into the Arctic Ocean. It is the world's second largest country by total area. It shares a common border with the United States to the south and northwest. Canada was formed in 1867 but was part of the Empire of Great Britain. However through acts of the British parliament in 1931 and 1982 it became independent of the United Kingdom. Canada today comprises of ten provinces and three territories and has a population of over 31 million.

BROTHER ANDREW

Andrew van der Bijl was born in 1928 in Alkmaar, Holland. When Andrew was eleven years old his country was invaded by the German army as the Second World War began. Life was very difficult for the next five years. He could no longer go to school and he and his family were treated badly. After the war Andrew became a soldier. He enjoyed the danger and the chance to travel to Indonesia. But he was badly wounded and spent much time in hospital.

In that hospital one of the sisters told him the good news of the gospel and Andrew was converted. When he recovered he returned to Europe, where he studied God's Word and attended Christian conferences. He was trying to discover what God wanted him to do with his life. When he was twenty-seven he visited Poland and was sadden by the suffering of the Christians there. The communist government had closed the churches and persecuted the Christians. So God gave Andrew an idea. Andrew could use his soldier and spy skills to smuggle in Bibles and Christian literature to God's people in the communist countries. Over the years God used Andrew to help encourage the church behind the Iron Curtain.

LOVING THE
ENEMY

AUGUST 1968

Disturbing images flickered across the television screen. 'Prague awoke today to Soviet tanks in their city streets and military planes in the skies,' the television presenter announced.

Andrew sat on the edge of his chair watching the news story report on the small screen in his sitting room in Holland. Tanks rolled through the streets as the Czechoslovakian people watched with confused and angry expressions. What was happening that caused the Russian government to send its soldiers to invade their friendly neighbour? Then Andrew had an even more serious thought. 'How will this affect my friends in the church there?'

In the years previous to this, Andrew van der Bijl had been busy helping Christians in countries controlled by the Soviet Union to receive Bibles and literature in their own languages. It was dangerous work because the Russian leaders were doing all they could to stamp out Christianity. Anyone caught reading a Bible, praying or worshipping God could be put in prison, beaten or even executed. Being a Christian in the Soviet Union was very difficult. For years Andrew had been smuggling Bibles into their country and secretly preaching there to encourage his Christian brothers and sisters.

Now sitting in his comfortable lounge surrounded by his wife and children, Andrew began to think about ways he could help in this new crisis. He already had lots of Bibles in the Russian language and literature written in the Czech language. So the obvious thing to do was take them to the people who needed them.

'You will be careful,' Corry, Andrew's wife, asked while she helped him pack up their big station wagon. Corry was used to Andrew travelling to many dangerous places but she still worried.

'Of course, I will,' Andrew replied. 'You just need to pray that the border guards and soldiers will not see the boxes of Bibles in the back of the car. God will take care of the rest.'

Andrew kissed his family goodbye and drove off with his precious load across Europe. Since the highways had no speed limits, Andrew drove as fast as his car could go and arrived at the Czechoslovakian border within a day. He knew that it was important to arrive while everything was still in confusion, before the Russian soldiers had managed to take complete control of the country. That way Andrew hoped he could slip in without much notice.

But when he pulled up to the border gate he was stopped by a guard carrying a machine gun. Andrew reached for his passport and prayed that God will let the soldier allow him into the country. As the man approached Andrew noticed how sad and defeated he looked.

'Don't you know what is happening here?' the guard asked Andrew, taking his passport.

'Yes, I know all about it,' Andrew replied.

'And you still want to come in? Look at all the people trying to leave!' and the guard pointed to the huge line of people, many in cars and on bicycles, waiting to cross the border out of the country.

'That is exactly why I want to go in, sir,'

The border guard shrugged and stamped Andrew's passport. He waved him through without even asking or checking what Andrew had in his car.

With so many people trying to leave Czechoslovakia the roads into the capital city of Prague were almost empty. Empty that is except for the Russian soldiers. Before Andrew reached the city, he came to a barrier set up by two large green tanks parked across the narrow road. Praying a silent prayer for God to keep the soldiers from seeing the Bibles, Andrew stopped the car once more.

Several soldiers armed with machine guns surrounded his car while one leaned down and pointed his gun at Andrew's head. Moving very carefully, Andrew handed out his passport to the man's waiting hand. The soldier looked at the passport briefly and nodded to his companions. Then the soldier withdrew his weapon, handed the passport back to Andrew and waved him to drive around the tanks. All of this happened without a word being spoken. Once Andrew drove around the tanks and he breathed out another silent prayer of thanks to God.

Arriving in the city of Prague, Andrew saw tank after tank rumbling through the streets. The tanks were so heavy that they tore up the paved and cobblestoned roads, making it difficult and dangerous to drive on.

Everywhere people stood on the streets in small groups, shouting or shaking their fists at the tanks and soldiers they carried. The Russians were not welcome and the Czech people were angry. But they were careful too. They didn't have any weapons to

fight the soldiers, tanks or military planes flying low in the skies. Andrew knew he had entered a war zone and his heart was pumping fast. He worried that a tank might just roll over his car and flatten it like a tin can, or that the soldiers would notice him driving by them with a Dutch registration plate and want to question him.

Driving through the city, Andrew came to the Vltava River that runs through Prague. As he drove across the bridge he glanced down the river at the many bridges that spanned the wide lazy river. Looking back as he arrived on the east bank he could see the many church spires gleaming in the fading sunlight. A beautiful city, he thought, if not for the military helicopters hanging in the sky above it. He turned onto a small street off the main road and found the address of some Christian friends. They were surprised to see him, but welcomed him into their home. They were amazed he would have come when the country was in such confusion.

'That is just why I came,' Andrew explained as the husband and wife sat down with him around their kitchen table with bowls of hearty soup. 'Once the Russians have closed your borders, no one would be able to get in. And I wanted to be able to see my brothers and sisters one more time before that happened.'

'You must come and speak in church tomorrow,' the husband urged. 'Before they close that down too. We have been so fortunate this last year with the government letting us meet. Now that will all change,' he finished sadly.

Andrew reached over and laid a hand on his friend's arm. 'But we know that God has not left you without hope. This is all part of his plan, even if we don't understand it just now.'

Andrew said nothing about the boxes he had in his car. He brought in only his suitcase and took the extra bed that his friends offered him.

The next morning, Andrew and his friends drove in Andrew's car through the streets still full of tanks and soldiers. Gunfire from here and there echoed off the stone buildings. How odd it was to see a huge modern tank standing in front of ornate stone buildings built five hundred years ago. The soldiers themselves were very young and looked worried and uncomfortable, especially when people yelled abuse at them or spat on them. Andrew said nothing, but an idea was forming in his mind. God gave him a message he wanted Andrew to share with the church in Czechoslovakia.

As they walked into the old church building, Andrew greeted the people he knew. They were surprised and overjoyed to see him.

'We thought no one would be able to get into our country now!' they said over and over. Andrew smiled and hugged each one.

When it was time to preach, Andrew climbed the steps up to the pulpit, asking God to give him the right words for his brothers and sisters in Christ.

'I know you want me to bring you words of comfort at this very unsettling time. Your country has been invaded and you are all at risk. However, I fear I must deliver words of rebuke instead.'

The congregation rustled a little and then fell silent. Only the sound of the shouts or rumbling tanks outside could be heard. And every now and then the windows rattled when some guns went off.

Andrew saw the people were puzzled, but willing to listen. 'You have enjoyed a time of freedom in your country. Your government has let you meet for worship without fear. And you have been allowed to travel without many restrictions. My friends you have wasted your time. What have you done with this precious freedom? Have you used it to go into Russia with Bibles and preach the gospel? No, instead you have made yourselves comfortable. You travelled to the west to buy new clothes, radios, and even cars. You have ignored your big brother in the east. And now the Russians have clamped down and your freedom is at an end.'

Andrew paused, letting his words sink in. The congregation were stunned, and then ashamed. Some bowed their heads, others began to cry.

After a few minutes, Andrew continued, 'But God had not turned against you. He loves you and he also loves the Russians. Since you didn't go to the Russians, God has brought them to you. Now you have the chance to give them the Word of God.'

That caught the congregation's attention. God had deliberately brought the hated Russian soldiers so that the Czech Christians could witness to them? But how?

Knowing what they must be thinking, Andrew smiled. 'God in his mercy has allowed me to come into Czechoslovakia with a special cargo. I have in my car boxes of Bibles in the Russian language. What better thing can you give a Russian soldier but God's Word in his own language!'

After the worship service, everyone crowded round to speak with Andrew. He opened up box after box, handing out the Russian Bibles to the eager Christians. He encouraged them to show kindness to the Russian soldiers, to show as well as tell about God's love.

Over the next few weeks, Andrew visited other cities around Czechoslovakia encouraging the Christians there to witness to the Russian soldiers too. The result was amazing.

The Russian soldiers had been told by their leaders that the Czech people would welcome them when they invaded their country, and they were shocked when people threw rocks at them and spat on them instead. No one in Czechoslovakia would help the soldiers in any way…not even to give them a drink of water. The soldiers were young and inexperienced. They were scared when they realized the Czech people hated them.

Then all of a sudden the Christians began to speak kindly to them. They offered them food and drink and told them that God loved them. They gave them Russian Bibles to read. The soldiers were surprised and pleased that someone was nice to them. So they accepted the Bibles and read them.

Soon the Russian leaders began to notice that their soldiers were becoming too friendly with the Czech people and not obeying their leaders' orders. Discipline among the soldiers was falling apart. So they recalled the entire army back to Russia and replaced them with older, more experienced men.

Czechoslovakia had to endure over twenty years of occupation. But the Christians knew God had worked a wonderful miracle in the midst of their suffering.

Where did those first Russian soldiers go when they were recalled? Back to their homes in Russia to share their Bibles and the gospel with their families and friends. God had used an invasion in Czechoslovakia to get Bibles into Russia, a country that had tried to keep God's Word out.

Devotional Thought:

*But love your enemies, and do good, and lend,
expecting nothing in return, and your reward will be
great, and you will be sons of the Most High, for he is
kind to the ungrateful and the evil. Luke 6:35*

Love your enemies. This is what Jesus told his disciples to do. And they were to do good to them. That was a difficult thing to hear because Israel was living under occupation too, just like the Czechoslovakians. The Roman soldiers were in charge. So those who loved God and wanted to obey him had to love those Roman soldiers even though they made their lives difficult.

Why did Jesus tell them and us to be kind to our enemies? Because God himself has been kind to us, offering us salvation when we were his enemies. So as God shows us love, we must show love to others.

Andrew was sent to Czechoslovakia to remind the Czech Christians about Jesus' command to love their enemies.

Andrew's mission called Open Doors International continues to deliver Bibles and literature to many countries around the world. There are two hundred full-time workers, and thousands of volunteers with offices in twenty countries.

Andrew himself has travelled to most of the places where Christians are persecuted, bringing help and encouragement.

COMMUNISM
FACT FILE:

T he continent of Europe was split between East and West after World War II. The West followed a Capitalist and democratic system of government while Communist countries in the East followed an economic structure and political ideology that meant that the state commonly owned all property and businesses – not the individual. Communism rejected religion and Christianity in particular, making Christians enemies of the state. The East and West entered a period called The Cold War – a state of conflict and competition that existed from the 1940s until the 1990s. A revolutionary wave of protests swept across Central and Eastern Europe in late 1989 ending the reign of communist states within the space of just a few months.

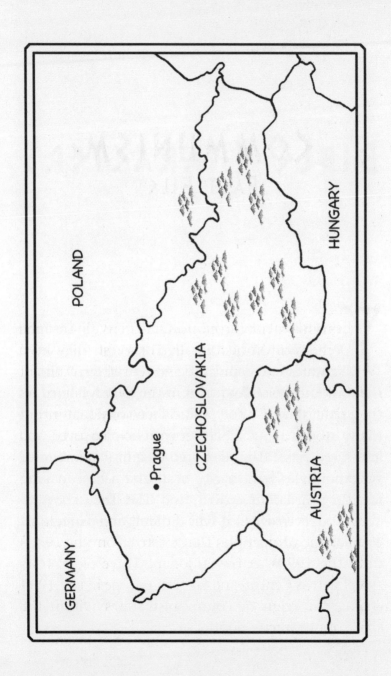

BIBLE CHARACTERS

You have now read four stories about men who lived in history. Even though they lived in different countries and at different times, they all loved God and took risks to serve him. As they studied their Bibles, those men would have read many stories about Biblical men who also loved God and faced risks. The next two chapters are about a governor who built a city wall and a deacon who faced a murderous crowd, and how they chose to obey God, even when it was difficult and dangerous. They are good examples for us too.

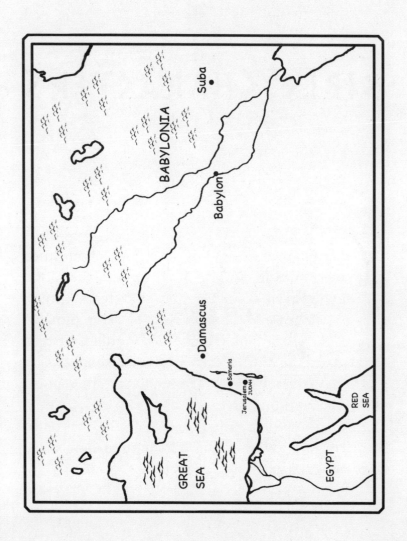

Suba

BABYLONIA

Babylon

Damascus

Samaria
Jerusalem JUDAH

GREAT
SEA

EGYPT

RED
SEA

NEHEMIAH, THE CITY BUILDER

NEHEMIAH 2-6

Do you like to be the leader all the time? Do you like to tell people what to do? Being the leader is fun sometimes, but it can also mean you have to listen to complaints and deal with difficult problems.

Nehemiah was chosen to be a leader for God's people and he had some difficult problems to sort out in a dangerous situation.

We read about Nehemiah in the book written by him in the Old Testament. At the beginning of his story Nehemiah tells us he was living in the city of Susa, the capital of Babylonia, and he worked for the king as his cupbearer. The people of Israel had been carried away from their homes and kept captive in Babylonia many years before. God had allowed this to happen as punishment for not obeying his commands. But as Nehemiah's story begins we learn that God has caused the king of Babylonia to let some of the Israelites return home and he sent Nehemiah too, as governor of Jerusalem.

The first thing Nehemiah did when he arrived in Jerusalem was to inspect the city. He did this at night when everyone was sleeping.

> I went out by night by the Valley Gate to the Dragon Spring and to the Dung Gate, and I inspected the walls of Jerusalem that were broken down and its gates that had been destroyed by fire. Then I went on to the Fountain Gate and to the King's Pool, but there was no room for the animal that was under me to pass. Then I went up in the night by the valley and inspected the wall, and I turned back and entered by the Valley Gate, and so returned. Nehemiah 2:13–15.

You can imagine how sad Nehemiah was to see the city walls and gates in such bad shape. The Jerusalem that King David and King Solomon had built was no longer beautiful or secure. But Nehemiah had a plan, a plan that God had given to him to carry out.

The next day Nehemiah called together all the important officials in the city. Some were nobles, some were priests and some were people who ran the local government. Nehemiah started by telling them something they already knew...Jerusalem was in ruins and needed to be rebuilt. And then he told them his plan.

"Come, let us build the wall of Jerusalem, that we may no longer suffer derision." And I told them of the hand of my God that had been upon me for good, and also of the words that the king had spoken to me. Nehemiah 2:17b-18a.

The people must have been relieved to hear that the king of Babylonia himself had allowed Nehemiah to come and rebuild their beloved city. They knew that their city was open to attack by their enemies lurking around them. So they answered Nehemiah immediately with 'Let us rise up and build.' Nehemiah 2:18b.

Nehemiah was encouraged to see the people so enthusiastic. He organized the work parties by families, giving each family a particular place at the wall or on a gate to work. Nehemiah even made a list that you can read in Nehemiah 3 so that everyone would know who the good workers were.

It was hard work and everyone from the youngest to the oldest in each family was expected to help. Men gathered up the large fallen stones. Children gathered up smaller rocks to place in the chinks between the large rocks. Women mixed up mortar to cement the stones in place. Trees had to be cut down in the nearby king's forest, carried up the hill and into the city, and then turned into huge gate posts and enormous wooden doors to be hung between them. Each day Nehemiah walked or rode his donkey around the city, encouraged to see the people working hard and with joy. Nehemiah urged them on reminding them that this was a good work for God.

But while the people were hard at work, so were their enemies. Nehemiah had suspected there were traitors in the city. He had told only the people of the city the plans to rebuild the city walls, but within a week their enemies arrived on horseback and stood with their soldiers to watch the people work. Sanballat, the governor of Samaria, Tobiah the Ammonite governor and Geshem the Arab started to jeer at Nehemiah and the people saying, 'What is this thing that you are doing? Are you rebelling against the king?' Nehemiah 2:19b.

Sanballat didn't want to see Jerusalem rebuilt. He wanted to be the most powerful governor in the area and he wanted Jerusalem for himself. So he thought he could frighten Nehemiah and the people by accusing them of rebelling against the king.

Nehemiah had a courageous answer ready. He told Sanballat that he had the king's permission and then he added, 'The God of heaven will make us prosper, and we his servants will arise and build, but you have no portion or right or claim in Jerusalem.' Nehemiah 2:20.

With those words he told his enemies and the people of Jerusalem that God was in charge of this building project. How the people must have cheered at the reminders that God was on their side. So they returned to their work with enthusiasm, while their enemies rode away. But more trouble was to come.

This time instead of threatening Nehemiah and the people directly, Sanballat and his friends tried another way to frighten the people into stopping their work. The people had been working very hard and soon the wall had been built to half its original height. Everyone in Jerusalem was pleased, but at the same time they knew it was not enough. Their enemies could still climb over those walls and get through the places where the gates had not been finished. At that point Sanballat sent people into the city to secretly start stories and rumours. These traitors whispered that Sanballat's soldiers were planning a sneak attack and they would kill everyone who was building the wall.

So the people went to Nehemiah to complain and ask what he was going to do to stop the sneak attack. None of them would go back to building the wall until Nehemiah did something. Nehemiah acted immediately. He stationed men with weapons at all the weak points in the wall. Then he called the rest together to reassure them and outline a plan. He told all the families to go back to work and to bring whatever weapons they had. They should keep those weapons close by and be ready to use them. He appointed one man to be a lookout and if he saw any threat to the city or the people he was to blow the trumpet. Then all the people would put down their tools and pick up their weapons, and be ready to fight. He said, 'Do not be afraid of them. Remember the Lord, who is great and awesome, and fight for your brothers, your sons, your daughters, your wives, and your homes.' Nehemiah 4:14b.

Nehemiah must have found being the leader very hard work in such a difficult and dangerous time. He had to be wise and make good plans to keep the people and the city safe. He also had to keep the people encouraged and not become discouraged himself. And the best way he could do that was to pray. He would take his troubles and concerns to God and ask for help.

Because the people worked hard, the walls climbed higher and higher until they were at last finished.

Now only the heavy gates had to be put into place and the city would be secure against their enemies. The people must have been tired, working all day and guarding the walls by night. They had completed the walls around the entire city in just fifty-two days.

But the threats were not over. Once more Sanballat and his allies tried to trick Nehemiah. They sent letters to him, trying to get him to leave the safety of the city and meet to talk about a peace treaty. But Nehemiah would not be lured away. He replied, 'I am doing a great work and I cannot come down. Why should the work stop while I leave it and come down to you?' Nehemiah 6:3.

Four times Sanballat sent letters and four times Nehemiah said no. So the fifth time Sanballat sent his servant with an unsealed letter that he showed to everyone he met on his way to give it to Nehemiah. It said, 'It is reported among the nations, and Geshem also says it, that you and the Jews intend to rebel; that is why you are building the wall. And according to these reports you wish to become their king. And you have also set up prophets to proclaim concerning you in Jerusalem, "There is a king in Judah." And now the king will hear of these reports.' Nehemiah 6:6-7.

Nehemiah sent a letter back saying that Sanballat was telling lies and the people wouldn't stop their work. Nehemiah also prayed and asked God to continue to strengthen his hands for the work. And God answered his prayer. Very soon afterwards the gates were hung in place and Jerusalem was secured against its enemies. The Bible says, 'So the wall was finished .... And when all our enemies heard of it, all the nations around us were afraid and fell greatly in their own esteem, for they perceived that this work had been accomplished with the help of our God.' Nehemiah 6:15-16.

God had turned the tables on his enemies. They were now afraid of Nehemiah because God was on his side. Nehemiah had a tough time as the governor of Jerusalem during that dangerous time, but God gave him wisdom and courage to do the job and kept him and the Israelites safe.

STEPHEN SPEAKS OUT
ACTS 6-7

Have you ever had to tell someone they are doing something wrong? Or has someone ever told you that you had behaved badly? None of us likes to hear that sort of thing. But sometimes people need to be told, especially when they are speaking against God or disobeying his law.

Stephen, a leader in the early church, had to tell some people their ideas about God were wrong and it cost him his life. We may never face death for our belief in God, but we do need to follow Stephen's example. We need to have the same courage Stephen had to speak up for God's truth. We read his story in Acts 6 and 7.

The time of the early church happened just after Jesus left this earth and returned to heaven. Before he left, he instructed his disciples to: 'Go therefore and make disciples of all nations, baptizing them in the name of the Father and of the Son and of the Holy Spirit, teaching them to observe all that I have commanded you.' Matthew 28:19-20a.

So the disciples gathered in Jerusalem to pray. And then they began to preach and teach and many, many people were converted. The disciples were also given the power to heal the sick and do other wonderful things. It was a very exciting, joyful time as the early church grew and grew. But it was also a difficult time.

The priests and leaders in the temple became angry with the disciples for teaching that Jesus was God's Son because they were the ones who had put Jesus to death. They had refused to believe who Jesus was or that he had come back to life again. So they arrested those who preached about Jesus, put them in prison for a short time and beat them. But as soon as the disciples were released, they went right back to preaching about Jesus, even though they knew they could be arrested again.

There were also some problems in the church. With so many people being converted, there were some who needed help; poor women whose husbands had died and they had very little money to buy food and clothes.

The church leaders quickly realised that they needed to appoint some leaders to take care of people in need. So they looked for men who loved God, and appointed a man called Stephen along with six others. The Bible describes Stephen as 'a man full of faith and of the Holy Spirit' Acts 6:5b.

We are also told: 'Stephen, full of grace and power, was doing great wonders and signs among the people.' Acts 6:8.

Stephen must have been a busy man. He, along with the other men, visited the homes of the Christians in Jerusalem, taking up a collection for the poor each week. Then he and the others would purchase food for the poor and deliver it to them. He also made time to pray, preach and heal people. Stephen was a hard worker for God.

The temple priests and leaders began to notice what Stephen was doing and challenged him to a debate. They hoped that they could show the people that Stephen was teaching wrong ideas about God. They tried to argue with Stephen against Jesus' teachings, But they began to look for another way to stop him because they 'could not withstand the wisdom and the Spirit with which he was speaking.' Acts 6:10.

They arrested Stephen and brought him to the temple for a trial. They hired people to accuse Stephen of saying terrible things against Moses and God. The false witnesses said, 'This man never ceases to speak words against this holy place and the law, for we have heard him say that this Jesus of Nazareth will destroy this place and will change the customs that Moses delivered to us.' Acts 6:13b-14.

Imagine how you might have felt if you had been Stephen. It was a fearful thing to be on trial before the high priest. But God gave Stephen peace in his heart and just the right words to say.

Stephen answered their accusations with a story. He told them the story of Israel, God's chosen people. They all knew the story well and loved to hear it. Stephen reminded them of how God had called Abraham to come to the Promised Land, how he had promised Abraham he would have many, many descendants even when Abraham had no children. God then gave Abraham and Sarah a son, Isaac, who then became the father of Jacob, who became the father of twelve sons. All the people of Israel could trace their family history back to those twelve men. But Stephen didn't tell that story just to remind them of their history. He wanted them to remember that God had chosen his people, had made promises to them and, most important, had kept those promises.

Stephen continued with his story. He told them about Joseph being sold as a slave in Egypt and God using him to help Pharaoh and then being allowed to bring God's people into Egypt during a famine. Then Stephen moved on to the story of Moses. Moses was the man the people of Israel loved and revered most because he had been so close to God and had given them God's law. Stephen reminded them how God had kept baby Moses safe and how he had grown up in the Pharaoh's palace. Then he described how Moses had run away from Egypt and God called him back, speaking from a burning bush. Moses obeyed and returned to lead God's people out of Egypt and back to the Promised Land.

As Stephen continued to mention Joshua, David and Solomon, the priests and leaders must have wondered why Stephen was telling them all this. They knew Israel's history just as well as he did. Then Stephen came to his final points.

First he told them that God doesn't just dwell in the temple. Solomon built the temple long after God had spoken to Moses from the burning bush or on

Mount Sinai. God didn't need a temple to speak to his people. And then he finished with his final point.

> You stiff-necked people, uncircumcised in heart and ears, you always resist the Holy Spirit. As your fathers did, so do you. Which of the prophets did your fathers not persecute? And they killed those who announced beforehand the coming of the Righteous One, whom you have now betrayed and murdered, you who received the law as delivered by angels and did not keep it. Acts 7:51-53.

The priests and leaders must have been stunned by Stephen's closing remarks. He had just said that they didn't obey God's law and had murdered the Messiah, the Righteous One, sent from God. Those were terrible accusations, and all the more so because they were true. But the priests and leaders wouldn't admit that. Instead they became very angry and started shouting.

At this point Stephen could have tried to back down. He could have said he was sorry for saying such things and promised not to do it again. But then he would have betrayed Jesus and turned away from the church. Instead he stood strong while all the men around him grew more and more angry. God gave him a vision to help him not to be afraid.

> But he, full of the Holy Spirit, gazed into heaven and saw the glory of God, and Jesus standing at the right

hand of God. And he said, "Behold, I see the heavens opened, and the Son of Man standing at the right hand of God." Acts 7:55-56.

When Stephen said that, the leaders and priests put their hands over their ears. They didn't want to hear any more. Then they lunged forward, grabbed Stephen and dragged him out of the temple, through the streets of Jerusalem and out one of the city gates. They threw Stephen down into a large pit and began to gather large stones and rocks to throw down on him. They took their coats off, giving them to a young man named Saul to take care of. Then they rolled up the sleeves of their tunics and began to throw the stones and rocks at Stephen.

Stephen didn't try to get away. It would have been impossible with the angry crowd surrounding him. So he used the last few minutes of his life to pray.

And as they were stoning Stephen, he called out, "'Lord Jesus, receive my spirit.' And falling to his knees he cried out with a loud voice, 'Lord, do not hold this sin against them.' And when he had said this, he fell asleep." Acts 7:59-60.

Even as he was dying, Stephen asked that God would have mercy on the very people who were killing him.

Once Stephen lay dead in the pile of rocks, the leaders and priests must have thought that they had won.

After all, Stephen would never again preach about Jesus or be there to accuse them of not following God's law. Stephen's life was over and he hadn't convinced them about Jesus. Stephen had failed. But just when we think of something as a failure God has a way of changing that into a success.

Remember the young man named Saul who was at Stephen's stoning? Remember how he took care of the coats belonging to the priests and leaders? Saul saw and heard everything that went on that day. Saul loved God more than anything else and he wanted to serve God with his whole life.

At first he thought the priests and leaders had been right to kill Stephen just as they had been part of killing Jesus, and he began to help them persecute the Christians. But God had other plans for Saul.

Saul must have remembered Stephen's sermon and actions. And when God called Saul on the road to the town of Damascus and told him to stop persecuting the church, Saul was converted. God had a big job for Saul to do.

So sometimes when it is hard to stand up for what is right, remember Stephen. We probably won't have to die as Stephen did, but we might have to listen to angry words or laughter at our 'religious' beliefs.

Remember to ask God for strength to do what is right. Not only will you please God, but you never know who else is watching, someone you might influence for good.

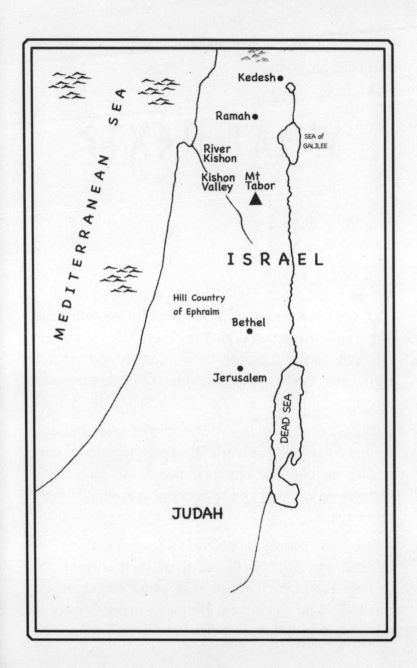

WHAT NEXT?

You have now read about six men who took risks to served God. They were all in some sort of danger because they chose to do what is right even if other people tried to tell them they were wrong.

They are a wonderful example of how to serve God even when it is difficult. You may never have to face such big dangers as they did, but each one of us who serves God and speaks out for what is right takes a risk.

We risk people laughing at us or making life difficult for us. But just as these men trusted God to help them, even when they were afraid, so we can trust God to help us. He has promised never to leave us or forsake us. When we call on him he will answer. Are you ready to take the risk of following God? Even if none of your friends or family do? God has promised us great blessing when we serve him as we should.

RISKTAKER QUIZ

Martin Luther

1. What did Martin Luther promise God when he was young?

2. What was the name of the Emperor?

3. What was the Elector of Saxony also known as?

4. Martin Luther knew that Salvation only comes from what?

5. When Martin was in hiding what name was he given?

RISKTAKER QUIZ

David Brainerd

1. What sad thing happened to David when he was still a young boy?

2. How old was David when he became a Christian?

3. Who was David a missionary to?

4. Who travelled with David Brainerd on his journey?

5. What was one difference between the Seneca Indian's religion and Christianity?

RISKTAKER QUIZ

William King

1. In what country was William King born?

2. What did his family do when he was 20?

3. What sad thing happened to William when he was in Edinburgh with his young family?

4. Who did William want to be more like?

5. What country did the slaves travel to?

RISKTAKER QUIZ

Brother Andrew

1. What is Brother Andrew's real name?

2. What happened to his country of Holland when Andrew was just eleven years old?

3. What did Andrew smuggle?

4. What is the name of the city that Andrew travels to in the story?

5. When the Russians invaded what were the people of Prague able to do that they hadn't done before?

RISKTAKER QUIZ

Nehemiah

1. What city was Nehemiah living in?

2. What was his job there?

3. What had happened to Jerusalem?

4. What did Nehemiah tell the people of Jerusalem to do?

5. When the walls were rebuilt all the nations knew that someone had helped Nehemiah and the people. Who was that?

RISKTAKER QUIZ

Stephen

1. In what Bible chapters do we read Stephen's story?

2. What was Stephen full of?

3. When he was being killed who did Stephen see when he looked up?

4. What people did Stephen pray for when he was dying?

5. Who looked after the coats of Stephen's attackers?

RISKTAKER QUIZ
ANSWERS

MARTIN LUTHER
1. He promised to become a monk
2. Emperor Charles V
3. Frederick the Wise
4. Faith in God
5. Knight George

DAVID BRAINERD
1. His parents died
2. 21
3. North American Indians
4. Eliab Byram, two guides and Tattamy the interpreter
5. The Indians worshipped many gods but the truth of Christianity is that there is only one true God

WILLIAM KING
1. Northern Ireland
2. They emigrated to America
3. His wife and children died
4. Jesus Christ
5. Canada

BROTHER ANDREW

1. Andrew van der Bijl
2. Germany invaded
3. Bibles
4. Prague
5. They could tell the Russians about Jesus and give them Bibles

NEHEMIAH

1. Susa in Babylonia
2. Cup-bearer to the king
3. The walls were broken down and the gates destroyed by fire
4. Rise up and build
5. God

STEPHEN

1. Acts 6 and 7
2. Grace and power and the Holy Spirit
3. The Son of Man (Jesus)
4. His enemies/attackers
5. Paul

GLOSSARY

Castellan – The caretaker of a castle

Cicadas – A large noisy insect with transparent wings. It usually lives in tropical areas

Colonial – A period of American history from the 1600s to 1776

Congregation – A group of worshippers in a church

Converted – When someone is changed from being an unbeliever to being a believer in Jesus Christ

Cup-bearer – A servant who drank from the king's cup in order to check for poison

Doctrine – A collection of beliefs or instructions. Christian Doctrine is the truths that the Bible teaches; the teaching and explanation of the word of God

Doublet – A snug fitted jacket

Emigrate – This is when you leave the country you were born in to settle in another

Faith – When we believe and trust in God to forgive us for our sins and save us

Gospel – The good news of Jesus Christ

Herald – Messengers sent by noblemen or royalty to convey messages and proclamations

Hose - Clothing worn on the legs

Imperial - This term is used when someone or something belongs to or is in charge of an empire

Massa - A word used by slaves instead of Master

Monastery - A building where monks live

Persecuting - When Christians were hurt or killed for their beliefs

Plantation - A large farm or estate in the tropics used to grow sugar, tobacco, cotton or coffee. In the past they have been associated with slavery

Pope - The man in charge of the Roman Catholic Church

Presbytery - A group of men who were elected by people in the congregation to govern the church

Priest - Someone with authority in a religious order

Scalp lock - A tuft of hair or long ponytail on the top of the head of a warrior. The rest of the head is shaved

Temple - A place of worship in Old Testament times

Tonsure - A special hair cut for monks

Weskits - A waistcoat

Wharf - A landing place or pier for ships

Witness - What Christians do when telling others about Jesus Christ

WHO IS LINDA FINLAYSON?

Linda Finlayson is a Canadian living in the USA in the area of Philadelphia. She has enjoyed working with children in schools, churches and children's clubs. Bringing together her love of books, children and history has given her the opportunity to write the adventure stories of real people.

Linda is married and has one son. She has also written *Wilfred Grenfell: Arctic Adventurer*.

STRENGTH AND DEVOTION

Linda Finlayson has written another book with stories of strength and devotion where we read about different women who took risks and faced dangerous situations for the glory of God. Katherine von Bora made a daring escape so that she could worship in freedom, Fidelia Fiske faced bandits and mobs in order to teach the truth, Amy Carmichael risked her life in order to help others live a Christian life, Lillian Dickson trusted God to help her cross some very dangerous jungle. Deborah lead an army when no one else had the courage. Jehosheba tricked a wicked queen in order to save the true king. These are the stories of real women who took real risks for God.

ISBN: 978-1-84550-492-2

RISKTAKERS

STRENGTH
AND DEVOTION

LINDA FINLAYSON

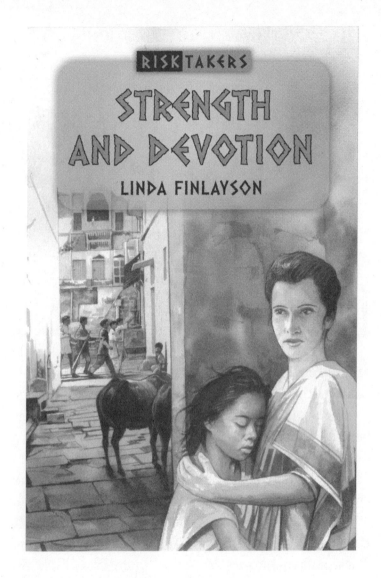

ISBN: 978-1-84550-492-2

STRENGTH AND DEVOTION
BY RITA FINLAYSON

Exciting stories, which will help young readers to discover the excitement of the Christian life.

Katherine von Bora escapes to freedom in a fish-monger's cart – all because she knows she must worship God as the Bible tells her to.

Fidelia Fiske and her students wait in baited breath as a terrifying mob attack the school. Teaching the children about Jesus has brought danger to her door.

Amy Carmichael helps a young woman escape her angry family under cover of darkness. Amy longs for all young Christians to be free to worship God in India.

Lillian Dickson swallowed her fears and went on a very dangerous trek up mountains and through forests in order to reach remote villages with the good news of Jesus Christ.

Deborah takes charge of an army when no one else has the courage.

Jehosheba risks her life to rescue her nephew. The throne of Israel and more is saved because of her actions.

These women were all willing to take risks. They faced danger and difficulties. Some faced great hardship because of what they believed in.

While reading their exciting stories you will learn about why they did what they did and who it was who helped them.

CHRISTIAN FOCUS PUBLICATIONS

Christian
Focus
Christian
Heritage
CF4K
Mentor

Christian Focus Publications publishes books for adults and children under its four main imprints: Christian Focus, Christian Heritage, CF4K and Mentor. Our books reflect that God's word is reliable and Jesus is the way to know him, and live for ever with him.

Our children's publication list includes a Sunday school curriculum that covers pre-school to early teens; puzzle and activity books. We also publish personal and family devotional titles, biographies and inspirational stories that children will love.

If you are looking for quality Bible teaching for children then we have an excellent range of Bible story and age specific theological books. From pre-school to teenage fiction, we have it covered!

**Find us at our web page:
www.christianfocus.com**

CF4•K
Because you're never
too young to know Jesus